The How to
be
JAMAICAN
Handbook

The How to be JAMAICAN Handbook

Written by:

The Jamrite Cultural Dissemination Committee
Kim Robinson, Harclyde Walcott & Trevor Fearon

The Jamrite Cultural Dissemination Committee consists of the following duly accredited experts:

Kim Robinson
Harclyde Walcott
Trevor Fearon

Cover Photo:	Peta Gay MacMillan
Cover Models:	George and Joanne
Cartoons:	Livingston McLaren
Illustrations:	Kim Robinson

November 1987 ....1st Printing
January 1988............................2nd Printing
May 1988.................................3rd Printing
February 1989..........................4th Printing
May 1990.................................5th Printing
December 1990.........................6th Printing
July 1991.................................7th Printing
January 1992............................8th Printing
August 1992.............................9th Printing

Other books by JAMRITE PUBLICATIONS

How to Speak Jamaican
Life in Jamaica
Ken Maxwell on Dis and Dat

A Humor Us™ Book

Jamrite Publications and Humor Us™ Books are divisions of Humor Us Publications.

Jamrite Publications,
14 Dominica Drive,
Kingston 5, Jamaica, W.I.

ISBN 976-8001-24-0

DEDICATION

Dedicated to those many Jamaicans,

here and abroad,

who have excelled internationally

in so many different fields . . .

and to all Jamaicans everywhere,

whose achievements may not

YET have been recognized,

but nevertheless

have no doubt whatsoever

that they're the greatest.

CONTENTS

Part I

The Cast Of Characters

THE JAMAICAN
POLITICIAN

The Jamaican Politician is a very interesting animal, and is unlike most others of the same species ("Animal Politico") found elsewhere in the world. Oh yes, he does the ritual shouting, when delivering his message to his people, and the requisite amount of shaking of hands is also there. But deep down there is an enormous difference: there is guts, often lots of it.

He is inherently hardworking, and zealously looks after the needs of his constituency. It is through this spirit that he is able to generate the arms and legs necessary to raise him to influential political office - a position that allows access to all kinds of ammunition with which to build the strength of his party.

The real strength of the Jamaican Politician lies in his sense of endeavour and enterprise. He demonstrates to his countrymen the true significance of the word "acumen", with his bewildering ability to maintain a "champagne" lifestyle on a "skyjuice" salary - a feat which amply qualifies him to be able to teach most of those M.B.A. graduates, who it seems can be found under every other rock, a thing or two about planning and finance.

Genius - sheer genius, that's what it is. Who else in this society is able to so convincingly demonstrate such economic growth? Who else is able to keep the nation's architects and builders in a constant flurry of activity? Come to think of it, he can teach the Government a thing or two.

THE PARTY HIERARCHY
The Boss, Leader, Wizard, Maximum Leader, Chief, etc:

Usually the elected Chairman of the Party; usually thought of as a genius in his/her youthful days, but as fate would have it by the time he/she arrives in office that designation has long since disappeared.

The possessor of this title must have one or several of the following:
a. loud voice
b. nervous twitch
c. a love for his/her own voice
d. great talent for the creation of acronyms
e. reputation as a ladies' man

The ideal boss surrounds him/herself with a group of people who rate between disciples and cheerleaders.

The Cheerleader:

This figure operates primarily in the House of Parliament and is responsible for leading the applause on cue - at every pause in the Boss's speech.

He can usually be seen with his open palm raised

3

about six to eight inches off the desk in a position of readiness. It is a position vied for by those interested in physical fitness and is reputed to lend to the development of the biceps.

The Chorus:

A cacophony of opinion-less voices . . . plays the role of supporting cast in Parliament. Very dependable, just needs to be pointed in the appropriate general direction.

The Hot Air Machine:

This post is usually reserved for a junior Minister; it requires that the holder of the title generate a considerable amount of hot air on subjects which are of no importance to the national interest. This individual is called upon particularly at Budget and IMF times. A true martyr.

The Runner:

Very adept at avoiding the Press - and/or any issue. Usually seen making swift departures. Usually reserved for Ministers of Labour.

The Sleeper:

This is a very interesting character. Always punctual, always present at all functions, can be seen at every Parliamentary session, but has only been heard to make two utterances in his twenty-five years in Parliament:

"Mr. Speaker, may I ask to have the air conditioning turned down."

"May I ask to have the window closed, the sun is in my eyes."

"Five pickney, $50, das all, fi pay rent, buy food, clothes, bus fare, school books . . . and yu wid all your education can't mek di money stretch?!!"

4

THE JAMAICAN POLITICAL SUPPORTER

Some Basic Guidelines

Middle class Socialists talk only to Middle class Socialists and upwardly mobile Democratic Socialists.

Democratic Socialists talk only to Middle class Democratic Socialists and upwardly mobile Socialists.

Right Wingers talk to Right Wingers.

Real upper class Socialists, Social Democrats, and Right Wingers talk only to their Brokers and Investment Bankers.

(Continued overleaf)

GRASSROOTS POLITICAL SUPPORTERS

Grassroots Socialists don't talk to Democratic Socialists.

Grassroots Democratic Socialists don't talk to Right Wingers.

Grassroots Right Wingers only talk to Right Wingers.

Real Grassroots Socialists, Grassroots Social Democrats and Grassroots Right Wingers don't talk to anybody.

How to be an Honest Jamaican Politician: Beats Us.

Grassroots Political Supporters

THE INFORMAL COMMERCIAL IMPORTER
(THE HIGGLER)

The un-named male of yesteryear who suggested that females are the weaker sex was obviously a humorist far ahead of his time. Consider if you will what he would have made of Boadicea's 20th Century heiresses, of the latter day Amazons. Consider this little nation where multiple thousands of women could, on their slowest days, out-Thatcher, out-Gandhi, out-Meir, Maggie Indira and Golda without working up a sweat.

Consider Jamaica's Informal Commercial Importers: but the latest manifestation

Yesterday's Higgler

of a long line of dominant women in Jamaica's history, descendants of Nanny, the fabled heroine of Jamaica's colonial days who could, with a twitch of her butt, deflect the bullets of hapless English soldiers, who could floor a man with her fingers, who could . . . well we could go on and on.

Today, there is not one Nanny. There are thousands. Like their matriarch, they too leave "strong" men crying in their wake, they too will never yield to domination by "so-so" man.

In basic terms, I.C.I.'s are traders. They buy and sell. They buy in Miami, Panama City, Port-Au-Prince, and a few other cities, and they sell their stock at flea markets, bend-down-plazas and in other assorted outlets throughout the island. Since the trade began to proliferate in the late seventies/early eighties, I.C.I.'s have moved up-market; no longer taking up yams to sell to finance six-for-99-cent drawers. Now, they're stocking "Miami Vice" wear, designer dresses, and are selecting which customers they'll supply,

8

using criteria as snob-consciously as any limp-wristed hairdresser. I.C.I.'s are rapidly becoming a new elite class, high-cost specialist suppliers who, awash in money, now own much of uptown Kingston through astute and cash-only investments.

SOME CHARACTERISTICS OF JAMAICAN HIGGLERS

Should you wish to enter the ranks of Jamaican higglers, the following are assets:

- Being female. Most higglers are women,

Long blonde video queen-styled hair (miraculously grown during one-week visit to Miami)

Solid gold jewellery

Luggage full of "personal effects"

Today's I.C.I.

and it is felt that certain talents associated with women, e.g. common sense, delight in bargaining, etc., are useful advantages.

- Being unmistakably female. Higglering is a robust occupation. The amply endowed frontally and in the rear are far likelier to endure (and triumph) in the pushing and shoving that takes place.

- Being of a forthcoming disposition. Higglering is not for the faint of heart or for the shrinking violet. In the course of a single day, a higgler may be required to stand up to stewardesses, customs officers, policemen, hotel employees, etc. etc., all of whom are conspiring to drive her out of business. Any higgler who allows herself to be intimidated might as well pack it in. Air Jamaica stewardesses, at long last, have met their match.

- Being physically fit: Higglering at the I.C.I.

level is a consuming occupation. A typical schedule may call for catching the 3:00 a.m./ 11:00 p.m. nightbird flight to Miami on a Thursday night, checking into a Miami dive (4 to a room, napping by rotation), hitting the streets from 7:00 a.m. till 11:00 p.m. on Friday and Saturday and heading home on Sunday.

- Being bilingual. Many higglers acquire bilingual skills which are useful in dealing with customs and immigration officials in other countries. Their importance lies in being able to understand what the official wants while communicating absolute ignorance if such is advisable. Many of these officials are in fact absolutely certain that Jamaicans speak no English. Indeed, after being subjected to a few choice forty-shilling words, they do have a point.

THE DRUG BARON

SCENE: The North Coast

A friend swears it's true: he was among the multiple hundreds on Turtle Beach in Ocho Rios over one holiday weekend when a yacht pulled up near the beach. He thinks it was a brand new craft, though, as he said, who cares if it wasn't. A yacht is, after all, a yacht.

So there he was on the beach, like several hundred others watching this yacht. One passenger (it later turned out that he was the owner) paraded around the deck, then clambered over the rails, balanced himself, executed a perfect dive and did not come up again.

Not, at least, of his own volition. It was only when a cute jerry-curled woman who was among those profiling on the yacht and who had squealed with admiration at the perfect dive and whose head had been bent over the side of the boat to chart the diver's progress, screamed, that any on yacht or beach realized that he had been down for quite a long time.

Frenzy erupted on the yacht. Two other men instantly hit the water. Cutie's screams subsided momentarily, while many on the shore waited for heads to rise above surface. Then Cutie's screaming began again. By this time a flotilla of sunbathers were swimming out to the yacht. The afore-mentioned friend, with the typical Jamaican concern for his fellow human, or fastness, was one of the earliest on the scene. Through the clear waters of Turtle Beach he could see clearly three men, the owner and two would-be rescuers some 18 feet down, drowning from the weight of gold chains, rings and dish-size pendants . . .

11

... On the way to work.

CHARACTERISTICS

Fleetness of Foot:

All the Jamaican drug barons are athletically inclined as is evidenced in police reports. Matter-of-fact testimony by the security forces have them outspeeding - on foot - helicopters, jeeps and other vehicles during raids. They have been seen to scale 15-foot walls, leap 20-foot gullies **and** accelerate.

Pragmatism:

Jamaican barons have a pragmatic outlook, a kind of c'est la vie attitude.

Invisibility:

Our drug barons remain unidentifiable despite years of arduous pursuit and investigation by our trustworthy police force.

Charity:

As many in our trustworthy police force will stress, were it not for the munificence of the drug barons, many of the police-men's offspring would be unable to attend the better high schools.

Discipline:

While the society, generally, has identified rampant indiscipline as a scourge on the nation, firm discipline is the hallmark of the operations of the barons. Underlings who have transgressed, in for instance not handing over receipts in toto, have even been spoken to in very firm tones. Some have died of heart attacks during such reprimands, but then that is only indicative of their being unused to insistence on honesty and integrity.

Civic Responsibility:

Ganja barons have a highly developed sense of civic responsibility. For instance they work closely with politicians and police men.

National Pride:

No self-respecting ganja baron would dream of shipping his produce by anything but Air Jamaica.

THE RANKIN

The Rankin is the fourth most powerful person in Jamaican society (after the Ganja Baron, Higgler and Politician - in that order). He was created by politicians in the 1970s, who generously provided him with first-class management training (often abroad), specializing in such useful areas as "Organizational Methods", "Strategic Planning" and "How to Win Friends and Influence People".

The Rankin has now emerged as Jamaica's most efficient and effective breed of manager. Unlike most others, the Rankin succeeds in maintaining control, getting things done and commanding respect all at the same time. He performs as Chief Planner, Projects Director and Financial Controller, reporting only to the M.P. - oops, sorry, we mean the M.D. (i.e. Managing Director). His organizational skills are unsurpassed. The Rankin sits in his Headquarters (usually the recesses of the corner bar) and controls the activities of all persons within, say, a six-block radius. The Rankin's use of communications technology is awe-inspiring in its efficiency (the Telephone Company should take note) - a stranger enters the Rankin's territory, and presto, within seconds his lieutenants are at the stranger's side.

Success of the Rankin's operations, and indeed retention of his seat of power, require discipline; and discipline is the Rankin's middle name (Exterminator, Terminator or Rambo might be the first). Watch how the Rankin's lieutenants quiver as they approach him.

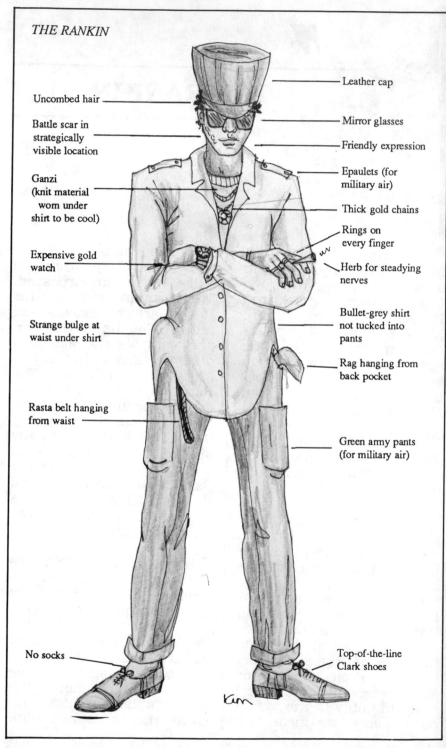

THE RANKIN

Uncombed hair

Battle scar in strategically visible location

Ganzi (knit material worn under shirt to be cool)

Expensive gold watch

Strange bulge at waist under shirt

Rasta belt hanging from waist

No socks

Leather cap

Mirror glasses

Friendly expression

Epaulets (for military air)

Thick gold chains

Rings on every finger

Herb for steadying nerves

Bullet-grey shirt not tucked into pants

Rag hanging from back pocket

Green army pants (for military air)

Top-of-the-line Clark shoes

One step wrong, they fear, may mean termination - of employment, of course. Do we blame them? High-paying jobs in Jamdown are hard to find these days!

HOW TO LOOK LIKE A RANKIN

- leather Clark shoes with no socks
- leather military-type cap
- jeans or army pants
- denim or army jacket over expensive knit shirt
- as many gold-capped teeth as possible (with at least one coloured, e.g. green, stone filling)
- as many thick gold bracelets and chains as possible

- mirror or very dark glasses
- wad of US$100 bills bulging in back pocket
- battle scars in strategic places.

HOW TO ACT LIKE A RANKIN

- don't smile (except when you're displaying the UZI or AK-47, about to fire, at which time such a dazzlingly friendly gesture is appropriate)
- don't walk - bop
- never raise your voice - be cool always
- never repeat an instruction
- drive a "rental".

THE JAMAICAN
CIVIL SERVANT

There is a species of individual among us who has been and continues to be a mainstay of our Society. This individual has been with us from the very beginnings of our nation-state: in actual fact, legend has it that when Columbus, "discovering" the island, stepped off his ship, he was greeted by an aged Arawak Indian bearing declaration forms in triplicate.

This species of individual is called the "Civil Servant". The Civil Servant prides himself on his ability to do four very important things and to do them well:

i.   to write legibly
ii.   to maintain his job for an excessively long period of time
iii. to be able to budget his salary with a skill that can only be described as miraculous
iv.   to maintain a firm belief in pride of position.

At this point let it be understood that the junior of this species usually tries to outdo his seniors when it comes to efficiency by:

i.   being forever busy
ii.   being constantly at lunch
iii. not being at his desk
iv.   consistently filling in for someone else: hence the constant use of the line "This is not my job", thus keeping the public constantly on its toes.

The Civil Servant benefits tremendously from this kind of beginning and later becomes quite an expert. Among his distinguishing features are:

i.   A concern for the term "length of service"
ii.   The need to receive his gold watch - inscribed of course - at the conclusion of his length of service
iii. A strong belief in his ancient means of transport-

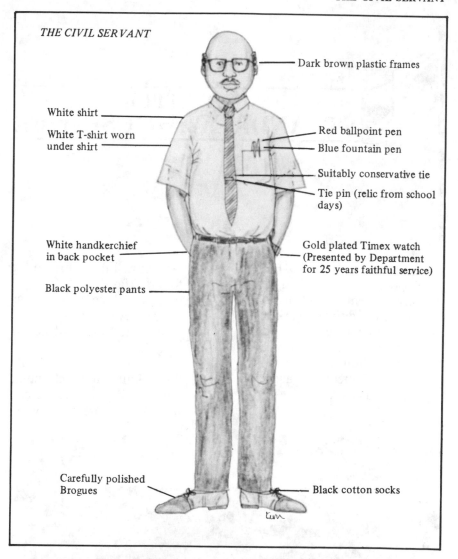

THE CIVIL SERVANT

Dark brown plastic frames

White shirt

White T-shirt worn under shirt

Red ballpoint pen

Blue fountain pen

Suitably conservative tie

Tie pin (relic from school days)

White handkerchief in back pocket

Gold plated Timex watch (Presented by Department for 25 years faithful service)

Black polyester pants

Carefully polished Brogues

Black cotton socks

ation (usually a hybrid of earlier model automobiles)

iv. The art of flowery handwriting even if used to say nothing

v. The ability to use selected Latin phrases from time to time, e.g. ad hoc, post factum.

It has also been documented that he especially looks forward to:

i. long leave
ii. study leave
iii. pre-retirement leave

but never has enough money to enjoy any of them; and as a result there develops a burning ambition to be able to reach retirement age so he can finally do something with his life.

THE UPPER
ST. ANDREW HOUSEWIFE

The Upper St. Andrew house-wife, poor soul, is often most unjustly condemned as being idle. Far from it! A diligent worker, an industrious woman, this poor maligned creature functions at a frantic pace from dawn till dusk, solving an incredible range of problems and crises, e.g.:

- what to tell the helper to fix for breakfast;
- what to tell the helper to put in Tracy Ann's lunch box;
- what to tell the gardener to do today;
- how to get it into the helper's thick skull that her cleaning, dusting, washing and ironing methods are entirely in-

Hard at Work

18

adequate without having to degrade oneself by actually **showing** her;

- how to fit in tennis, the hairdresser, the dressmaker, the PTA meeting and picking up the children from school all in one day;
- how to organize yet another fundraising tea party while overseeing the helper's preparation of refreshments for one's own tea-time guests;
- how to discuss critical issues with one's tea-time guests while overseeing the helper's preparation of dinner;
- how to be alluring, coquettish and delectable to one's husband while keeping a constant eye on the kitchen in order to catch the helper red-handed when she tries to sneak food into her bag before going home.

It should be noted that the Upper St. Andrew housewife has a very important function: that of supplementing the amount of information available and generally aiding the communication process with regards to matters of critical national importance. For example: whose husband slept with whose wife, whose husband slept with whose husband, whose wife slept with whose wife.

Such information is of course imparted over tea on the verandah *(see Verandah Talk)*.

Habitat:
Cherry Gardens, Norbrook, Barbican.

Appearance:
Usually light brown in colour; beady eyes; small chirping mouth which opens and shuts rapidly at tea parties, and curls into a sneer when the helper is being addressed.

Distinctive Features:
Speaks in a highly cultured tone with lots of "my dear's" and "darling's" interspersed.

Favourite Activities:
- Tea parties
- Going to the hairdresser
- PTA meetings
- Sitting on several committees to look into the nature of poverty
- Telling off the helper
- Discussing the shortfalls of today's helper with other Upper St. Andrew housewives
- Discussing the deep dark secrets of strangers, acquaintances and absent friends with whichever friends happen to be on one's verandah *(see Verandah Talk)*
- Lavish dinner parties where the hostess is lavishly praised after she modestly acknowledges that she single-handedly prepared every single dish.

Essential Criteria:
1. Must pay all helpers (e.g. cook, gardener, nanny, day's worker) as little as possible.
2. Must be able to fly to Miami every Friday to shop and have her hair done.

THE JAMAICAN YUPPIE
(The Young Urban Professional)

Yes, Virginia, we do have our yuppies. Some call them puppies (an unkind, and inaccurate, reference to alleged poverty, and not to lack of house training or personality of mothers). Buoyed somewhat by their superior outlook due to a superior cosmopolitan exposure from attending university abroad (which they're very proud of indeed), these yuppies have managed to sail smoothly into high-paying jobs by the time they hit 30. Jamaican yuppies must not be confused with the nouveaux riches *(see Drug Barons)* or ordinary middle-class Jamaicans *(see Real Men)*. Heaven forbid! Jamaican yuppies, you see, have Sophistication and Discriminating Taste, attributes which none but fellow yuppies would understand. After all, which other Jamaicans would go out of their way to watch movies in a language that they can't understand or to eat cheese that's full of fungus?

A PROFILE OF THE JAMAICAN YUPPIE

- Jamaican yuppies have Masters' degrees, preferably an M.B.A., obtained from an Ivy League American University.
- Jamaican yuppies have high-paying jobs, preferably in Marketing, Financial Analysis or Law.
- Jamaican yuppies drive company cars.
- Jamaican yuppies' favourite games are chess and trivial pursuit. They play chess. They live trivial pursuit. (Yuppies also occasionally play dominoes to be rootsish.) Jamaican yuppies plan to learn bridge one day - as soon as they've acquired their homes in Cherry Gardens or Norbrook.
- The minds of Jamaican yuppies are awesomely full of important details, e.g. the level of porosity in the

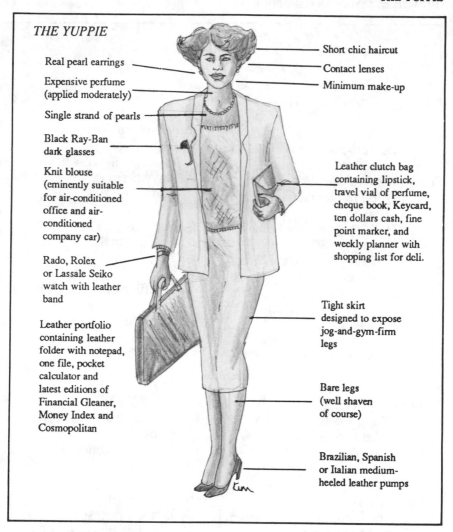

THE YUPPIE

- Short chic haircut
- Contact lenses
- Minimum make-up
- Real pearl earrings
- Expensive perfume (applied moderately)
- Single strand of pearls
- Black Ray-Ban dark glasses
- Knit blouse (eminently suitable for air-conditioned office and air-conditioned company car)
- Rado, Rolex or Lassale Seiko watch with leather band
- Leather portfolio containing leather folder with notepad, one file, pocket calculator and latest editions of Financial Gleaner, Money Index and Cosmopolitan
- Leather clutch bag containing lipstick, travel vial of perfume, cheque book, Keycard, ten dollars cash, fine point marker, and weekly planner with shopping list for deli.
- Tight skirt designed to expose jog-and-gym-firm legs
- Bare legs (well shaven of course)
- Brazilian, Spanish or Italian medium-heeled leather pumps

corks of the 1969 Chateauneuf du Pape, or the migratory habits of the dimple-eyed starfish - both hot subjects for discussion.

- Having already perfected their minds, Jamaican yuppies spend a lot of time trying to perfect their bodies, usually by jogging or going to the gym -wearing brightly coloured designer sportswear, of course. This activity is extremely important, as it allows one to profile successfully at Hellshire on Saturdays.

- Jamaican yuppies have children called Damien, Dominic, Sacha or Keshia Ann, who wear designer jeans, designer suits and designer booties from the age of 8 months.

21

RULES OF JAMAICAN YUPPIEDOM

Where To Go:
- Jazz concerts
- European Film Festivals
- Gloria's on the sidewalk (good for yuppie slumming excursions)
- Hellshire - the free beach
- Beaches in St. Ann
- Le Pavillon or Rivers Meet for tea on Friday
- For holidays: Europe, Latin America, the Far East
- Delicatessens
- Mona Dam for jogging
- New Kingston Mall

Where Not to Go:
- Reggae concerts
- Midnight movies
- Anywhere else for slumming
- Fort Clarence
- Beaches in St. Thomas
- Any Happy Hour
- Miami, New York, Toronto
- King Burger, Kentucky Fried
- Anywhere else for jogging
- Any other Mall

What To Wear:
- Old (or preferably new) faded jeans
- Natural fabrics

What Not To Wear:
- Dark blue skin-tight stretch jeans
- Synthetic fabrics

What To Do:
- Drink imported white wine, or gin or vodka
- Read The Economist, Money Index, Entrepreneur
- Invest in the stock market
- Be a Financial Analyst or Lawyer
- Aspire to live in Norbrook or Cherry Gardens

What Not To Do:
- Drink rum or scotch (absolute no-no: Red Label)
- Read the Star
- Play horses
- Be a Teacher, Nurse or Civil Servant
- Even consider living in Mona or Hope Pastures

THE HARD CARD

(UNDERSTANDING THE SENSITIVE, THOUGHTFUL, ALTRUISTIC JAMAICAN MALE)

No matter that the official census puts the Jamaican male: female ratio at approximately 1:1, the Jamaican male (and, surprisingly enough, many Jamaican females) knows that it is somewhere between 1:5 and 1:7 in his favour. He is therefore understandably annoyed at suggestions that his practice of, shall we say, dividing his attentions among a sizeable number of women is construed as an illustration of irresponsibility, fickleness, immaturity or rampant concupiscence.

Fair, he points out, is fair. All of God's children need, deserve love. Given a 1 to 5 (or 1 to 7) numerical disadvantage among Jamaican women, what Jamaican man possessing a modicum of thoughtfulness, charity, Christian concern even, would back off from his manifest duty to save our women from a loveless life? We all, he asserts sincerely, must pitch in and do the best we can. It's not an easy task, but it's one we are duty bound to give our best shot. It's a hard life, but someone has to live it . . .

So it is, that at 1:30 in the morning, legions of Jamaican men, footsoldiers in the war against loneliness, end their third shift of the day and wend their way home, dog-tired but glowing with a sense of patriotism, radiant with the satisfaction derived from a job well done . . .

A feeling marred only by their thoughtless wives who, unappreciative of their spouses' sterling role in preserving the social fabric and displaying no solidarity with the lot of their disenfranchised sisters, awaken to vindictively demand their, so to speak, pound of flesh.

It is not, he reiterates, an easy life. And such chauvinistic behaviour only makes it more difficult. Sometimes, he confesses, he comes close to chucking it in, but the thought of letting the side down, forcing some other man out there to shoulder an addi-

Agility: Required for ducking out of windows.

tional five or seven is not something he can contemplate without berating himself for selfishness. His only wish is that the wider society was more appreciative of his sacrifices.

UNSUNG VIRTUES OF THE JAMAICAN HARD CARD

Society's carping about the Hard Card's irresponsibility totally ignores the many commendable traits developed and enhanced by his selfless dedication to duty. These virtues include:

Managerial Skills (especially financial management):
Ability to run several households simultaneously.

Stamina:
Coping, on a day-to-day basis, with a range of physical demands.

Concentration/Creativity:
Ability to keep all the names straight and to conceive, on the spur of the moment, reasonable explanations eg. for absences. *(See Jamaican Excuses.)*

Sense of Family:
The Hard Card is, typically, fanatically devoted to his large family, many of whom live out in the country, many of whom drop in unexpectedly and need to be taken out to the supermarket or nightclubs. "Who is that woman I heard you were with at Turntable when you were supposed to be on a sales trip on the North Coast?" "Oh, that was my cousin and the last time I visited her family I had promised to take her out whenever she came to Kingston. It was so boring . . ."

Agility:
Required for ducking out of windows, and generally keeping out of the way of husbands and boyfriends.

THE HARD CARD
AS DEPUTY

Our thoughtful Jamaican male knows that many others of his sex, who share his selflessness, sometimes neglect to, as it were, keep the home fires stoked. As a gesture of solidarity with his brothers-in-arms, and conscious that it won't do to altruistically solve one problem while allowing another to develop, he sometimes offers his services as a deputy. Thus, his first shift may be at the home of someone doing a second shift elsewhere ... Often however, his gesture is not fully appreciated: not, mind you, out of any jealousy on the other man's part but simply because the other man might be so filled with self-reproach and doubt about his own ability to keep up his national duty that he may act irrationally. The wise deputy, after having breached the portal, identifies quickly the alternative exits.

Of course the deputy has no such fears at home, and to suggest that his tapping of his own phones, the reading of his wife's mail and his unexpected appearances at his own home indicate any such thing is to greatly misunderstand him. It is rather an indication of his care and love.

THE HARD CARD
AS FATHER

No man dares come to the Hard Card's home to visit his daughter. Fraternal solidarity after all only goes so far. On the other hand, his sons are tacitly encouraged to emulate his prowess.

SELF-ELECTED
HARD CARDS

- Politicians
- Athletes
- Musicians

Working out to keep up the stamina.

THE HARD CARD'S THEME SONG

Sophia George's *"Girlie Girlie"*.

HARD CARD'S COAT OF ARMS

Phallus dominant, rampant and levant, poised over maiden couchant.

HARD CARD'S TOOLS OF THE TRADE

- Unguents: Palm oil, Vaseline intensive care lotion
- Stimulants: Chinese brush, tantaria
- Drinks: Irish Moss, Front End Lifter

THE AGEING HARD CARD

Even with the wisest use of the above, the Hard Card must, alas, slip into the embrace of old age one day. It is a tragic sight. See him now in the dingy hotel, his false teeth resting in the glass of water, his slackened body unresponsive, his brain forgetting what he had set out to do. He is now a prime candidate for the ultimate putdown by ungrateful, unthinking women, the devastating "you soff"! For someone who has given his all to preserving the social order, this is a disgraceful abandonment by society. His only recourse is peer counsel and support through "Soft Card Anonymous", or tenure as a "Boops".

Inside the Hard Card's medicine chest.

THE BOOPS

Once a Hard Card but now justifiably exhausted after 20-plus years of being in the field, this fine fellow has decided to simplify his life-style. He is at the age where he can afford it. Once obliged to establish a professional reputation by racing around town, performing super-athletic feats with less than 4 hours sleep per night *(see Hard Card)*, he can finally relax. He has made it finan-cially; he has proven his worth as a Hard Card. It is now time for him to sit back and enjoy the fruits of his labour. Instead of chasing after ten women in any given period, he can reserve the pick of the crop for himself. A young, just-ripe, juicy nubile nymphet is the obvious choice.

So he dons his paisley-patterned silk shirt (it has served him long and well), tucks it into his polyester pants (a bit difficult to manoeuvre because of the paunch), steps into his white shoes, splashes on the Brut. Then finally adds the two items that are guaranteed to make him irresistible: the single thick gold chain around the neck and the diamond ring on the pinky. Then, an excuse to the wife about meeting the boys *(see Jamaican Excuses)*. Then, into the BMW. Off to the disco.

A score of nymphets are there, of course, all very eager. All he has to do is choose one.

After that, things happen fast. On the first date he pre-sents the nymphet with a bottle of French perfume. On the second date, the gold chain is offered. On date

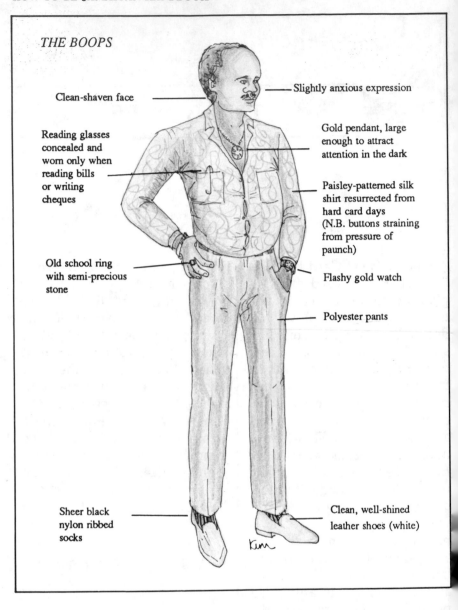

THE BOOPS

Clean-shaven face

Reading glasses concealed and worn only when reading bills or writing cheques

Old school ring with semi-precious stone

Sheer black nylon ribbed socks

Slightly anxious expression

Gold pendant, large enough to attract attention in the dark

Paisley-patterned silk shirt resurrected from hard card days (N.B. buttons straining from pressure of paunch)

Flashy gold watch

Polyester pants

Clean, well-shined leather shoes (white)

number three, the apartment that he has found her is discussed. A week after that, when he has moved her in, he now officially possesses his own Boopsie. All he has to do now is provide the rent money, grocery money, clothing allowance and entertainment allowance. For the services of a young sex kitten made available whenever needed, a small price indeed.

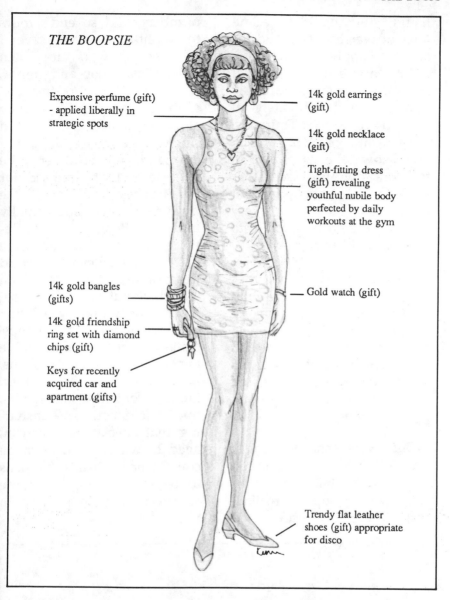

THE BOOPSIE

Expensive perfume (gift) - applied liberally in strategic spots

14k gold earrings (gift)

14k gold necklace (gift)

Tight-fitting dress (gift) revealing youthful nubile body perfected by daily workouts at the gym

14k gold bangles (gifts)

Gold watch (gift)

14k gold friendship ring set with diamond chips (gift)

Keys for recently acquired car and apartment (gifts)

Trendy flat leather shoes (gift) appropriate for disco

THE BOOPSIE

She has just turned 17, and is probably still in school. A fact of little import, because, being a smart girl, she has long since realized that what she learns at school will not help to get her where she wants to go.

So instead, she spends long

hours studying the techniques of weight-lifting and the art of applying make-up. Results are tested carefully at Hellshire every Saturday morning, and ultimately at the disco every Thursday, Friday and Saturday night. She knows she has to be in top condition, because there's a lot of competition out there. Remember, for every Boops there are at least 10 to 12 aspiring Boopsies.

A tricky business, this. Once preliminary negotiations with the Boops commence, the Boopsie must take care to play her cards right. After all, if she gives too much too early or too little too late, she might not get the contract.

But when she eventually cops a Boops, the Boopsie can relax. Not totally, however. The wise Boopsie realizes that there is safety in numbers, and so endeavours to contract with several Boopses - who are then ranked as major and minor, according to level of financial commitment, with time allotted accordingly. Be it a single or multifaceted arrangement, however, the Boopsie is to be praised for her forebearance: for if the truth be known, she actually finds her Boops to be somewhat less than exciting. Give her the challenging Hard Card or the macho Real Man any day! But she will persevere, bravely and unselfishly: for not only do the Boops' generous endowments solve her own financial problems, but also those of her mother, father, brothers, sisters, aunts, uncles and cousins - including that special male cousin, aged 22, who, by some strange coincidence, always happens to be at the Boopsie's home whenever the Boops pays a visit.

A few tokens of appreciation from the Boops.

THE BEAUTY CONTESTANT

Not everybody has what it takes to be a Jamaican beauty contestant. Good looks, a good shape, charm and some intelligence are of course advantageous, but what one really needs to be is **BRAVE**... (see page 34).

PREREQUISITES
- THE IDEAL CANDIDATE

Age:
Officially 18-25, unofficially 18-19.

Place of Birth:
Anywhere.

Place of Residence:
Anywhere, as long as you arrive in Jamaica in time for eliminations. (However, you must emphasize that you are Jamaican - preferably, but not essentially, in a Jamaican accent.)

Features:
Hair:
Long, preferably straight.
Skin Tone:
Light brown (the lighter the better, except for a sun-tan, which of course can be as dark as you wish).

Education:
Secretarial school or university. Florida university ideal.

Career Aspirations:
Bilingual secretary or model; civil engineer or model; astrophysicist or model; brain surgeon or model.

Interests and Hobbies:
Fashion shows, modelling, working out at the gym (n.b. (1) this is an essential pre-requisite; (2) not all gyms qualify), profiling at Hell-shire, testing perfume and make-up samples at the New Kingston shopping mall,

modelling (oh, did we say that already?).

Public Speaking Skills:

In the event that you are chosen to represent your country in an international contest, must be able to explain to the interviewer why everyone should visit your wonderful island ("We have beautiful beaches, warm and friendly people, and wonderful reggae music!").

If you don't satisfy any of the above criteria for the more popular contests, you may wish to consider a number of other options:

Miss Star Baby:
A good starting point for an illustrious beauty contest career.

Mini Miss Jamaica:
Ideal continuation of the training program.

Miss Jamaica Teenager:
Useful for those nymphets who haven't quite met the minimum age requirement for Miss Jamaica World/ Universe.

Miss Jamaica Mother:
All mothers eligible (ages 15 to 55).

Miss Jamaica Grandmother:
Must have at least two of her own teeth.

Miss Jamaica Farm Queen:
All young women with knowledge of pigs or cows eligible.

Miss Parish of Portland/ Clarendon/Manchester etc:
Ideal for those who can't afford the minibus fare to Kingston. Some knowledge of your parish would be an asset, but not essential.

Miss Jamaica Independence:
All independent women eligible (i.e. no boopsies allowed).

National Festival Queen:
"This is not a beauty contest." The organizers should know!

Miss Jamaica Bikini:
All women of all shapes and sizes eligible.

Miss Jamaica U.K./ Miss Jamaica U.S.A./ Miss Jamaica Miami:
For those who don't find it possible to spend a few months in Jamaica to enter Miss Jamaica World.

Miss City of Montego Bay:
For those who don't find it possible to spend a few months in Kingston to enter Miss Jamaica World.

Miss Jamaica Fashion Model:
All unsuccessful Miss Jamaica World contestants eligible.

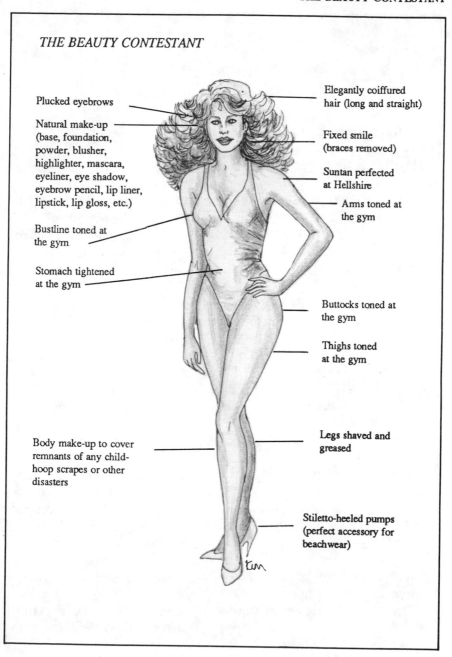

THE BEAUTY CONTESTANT

Plucked eyebrows

Natural make-up
(base, foundation,
powder, blusher,
highlighter, mascara,
eyeliner, eye shadow,
eyebrow pencil, lip liner,
lipstick, lip gloss, etc.)

Bustline toned at
the gym

Stomach tightened
at the gym

Body make-up to cover
remnants of any child-
hoop scrapes or other
disasters

Elegantly coiffured
hair (long and straight)

Fixed smile
(braces removed)

Suntan perfected
at Hellshire

Arms toned at
the gym

Buttocks toned at
the gym

Thighs toned
at the gym

Legs shaved and
greased

Stiletto-heeled pumps
(perfect accessory for
beachwear)

NOTE:

All of the above contest-
ants can look forward to
being kissed by the world's
number one patron of beauty
contests: Jamaica's Governor
General.

THE SCENE:

The Miss Jamaica Poolside Show

I have agreed to accompany a girlfriend who regularly attends these events.

I notice that most of the people around me are female ... and very fancily dressed females too. They all have on the latest fashions, are perfectly made up, and look as if they have just stepped out of hairdressing salons. All dressed to puss-back-foot - dressed to kill, even. Everybody looks quite excited and eager for the show to begin.

"Where are all the men?" I ask, perplexed.

"What men?" says my girlfriend blankly.

The show begins. The fun starts.

"Lawd a massy, a wha' dat?"

Or: "Woyoy!"

Or: "A who tell she fi enter? No, mi dear, you better drop out right now!"

Or: "Check de gal deh! Watch her knee dem how dem knock when she walk!"

And: "Eh-eh! But see yah! What a mawga foot gal!"

"Hey-hey, bwoy!"

"Look how her batty shakey-shakey!"

"But what dis one doing on the stage?"

"What a way her belly stick out! She gwine have baby?"

"Is where she buy dem clothes? Bendown Plaza?"

"Next time she must go to a dressmaker who like her."

It is easy to get caught up in the rating game. "I like that one," I venture at one point.

"Who, she?" says a stranger to my right. "Why she never comb her hair before she come out on the stage?"

"This one has a pretty face," I say later on, when I feel brave enough again.

"Yeah, but her leg dem well flabby like jell-o," says a pretty young miss in front of me.

And, yes, I confess: "This one going make the top five," says Susan authoritatively.

"Who, her?" I exclaim. "But look how she lang-i la la!"

All in all the entertainment is first-class.

THE REAL MAN

(a.k.a. The Reluctantly Uptown Footballer)

ORIGIN:
Usually middle class (a sad truth which the Real Man tries his best to conceal), often university educated (usually at the University of the West Indies).

AGE:
Late twenties to late thirties (over this age you're ineligible because you're too old to play football, under this age you're probably ineligible because your values are warped - e.g. liking music other than reggae).

SEX:
Very definitely male.

COMMON NAMES:
Mikey, Junior, Bigga, Robbo, Chalo, Panno, Mello, Dello, etc.

APPEARANCE:
Powerful, muscular legs (due to playing football), skinny shoulders and arms (due to doing nothing but playing football), small pot belly (due to drinking copious quantities of Red Stripe after playing football).

HABITAT:
Most easily found at any football field. During working hours, try the marketing division of any business place. At night-time, a good bet is a reggae club (the Real Man is the creature standing in a dark corner, leaning against the wall in a line with a posse of other Real Men, Red Stripe bottle in hand).

DISTINCTIVE CHARACTERISTICS:
Speaks like the average educated person from midnight to 5:00 p.m. on a normal working day, but from 5 to 12 (and all day on weekends) takes on a rootsish drawl, particularly effective when uttering philo-

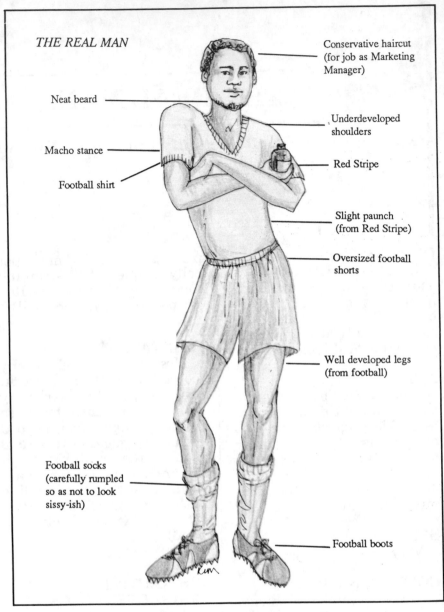

THE REAL MAN

Conservative haircut
(for job as Marketing
Manager)

Neat beard

Underdeveloped
shoulders

Macho stance

Red Stripe

Football shirt

Slight paunch
(from Red Stripe)

Oversized football
shorts

Well developed legs
(from football)

Football socks
(carefully rumpled
so as not to look
sissy-ish)

Football boots

sophical profundities to a
fellow Real Man, e.g.:
  "So wha de man a seh?"
  (Hi! How are you doing?)
  "Inna de struggle, you no
  see it?"
  (Just great.)
  "Level vibes."
(I'm glad to hear it.)
"Well, right now I man a
trickle."
(See you.)
"Cool runnin's."
(Bye.)
"Seen."
(Bye.)

FAVOURITE CLOTHING:

(Suitable for most leisure-time activities): Any t-shirt, football shorts, any thick socks, football boots. (These articles of clothing are, when the owner is obliged to wear less favoured apparel, always kept in the car trunk, just in case.) Note that it is against the basic principles of the Real Man to wear clothes that may be interpreted as "Trendy". Trendiness is effeminate. No way is a Real Man going to look effeminate.

FAVOURITE COLOURS:

Anything except pink.

INTERESTS:

Football, reggae, women, dominoes and football.

MATING HABITS:

Difficult to record, as the Real Man, who understands fully that the woman's place is in the kitchen, the bedroom, or looking after the little yout' dem, hardly goes anywhere with her. However, close surveillance may reveal the Real Man discreetly entering the home of one of a number of young ladies after dark. What he does inside is anybody's guess. Discuss football, perhaps? *(See Hard Card.)*

OFFSPRING:

The Real Man's primary concern is to produce little footballers.

DIET:

All traditional Jamaican food, e.g. curry goat, stew peas, mackerel rundown, mannish water. All traditional Jamaican put-it-back drinks, e.g. Dragon, Mackeson, Red Stripe, Irish Moss, Stagga Back, Front End Lifters. No foreign foolishness except chop suey and sweet and sour **chicken** (washed down with Red Stripe, of course).

SAMPLE MENU FOR A TYPICAL WORKING DAY

Breakfast:
Ackee and saltfish, green bananas, fried dumpling, Horlicks.

Lunch:
2 patties and a Dragon.

Dinner:
Cowfoot, rice and peas, yam, coco, yampi, dasheen, sweet potato, fried plantain, cole slaw.

Late Night Snack:
Half a jerk chicken, plus Irish Moss or 2 Red Stripe (n.b. not Stripes) - bought on the way home from a night out with the Posse.

THE NORTH COAST
HUSTLER

Any tourist in any country in the world will encounter variants of this species. Of course, the Jamaican varieties, by virtue of being Jamaican, are particularly colourful. For instance, the prostitutes that hang around resort areas, in a superb demonstration of marketing skill, will offer such exotics as the "Round-the-World", the "Screwdriver", or the "Pepper Steak", backed up, of course, by such standards as the "Roast Duck". The ganja dealer, quietly self-assured in the superiority of his product, need only breathe "Sensi" or "Lamb's Breath" to communicate, even when he is really selling "bush". The itinerant craft vendors, clutching carvings of Rasta heads and wooden figurines of fantastically endowed males, are in one shot covering two areas of some real and perceived renown.

Reigning supreme however, is the male hustler whose product is himself. He is easily recognizable. Almost inevitably, he wears locks, has a trim figure (quite often with a few knife scars), carries an ornately carved stick and is a walking collection of gifts from happy clients: chains, rings, Gap and Banana Republic jeans and t-shirts, and Nike, Adidas or Reebok sneakers, as well as Sony Walkman or ghetto blaster.

Neophyte hustlers are wont to offer their services overtly and clumsily. Displaying incredible gaucherie, they are apt, early in the mornings, to jog slowly along the beach clad in G-string-like wear, slowly enough so that their expertise in isolating

A north coast hustler in action.

muscle movements may be discerned. There is, to be sure, a market for those who subscribe, uncreatively, to the Truth-in-Advertising ethos.

The experienced ones are different. They sit around just looking cool and virile. At all beaches where they are able to reach an accommodation with security men, you will see them in the background, shirt off to reveal a firm and lightly muscled midriff (with, as noted, a few racy scars), and there, enigmatic behind mirrored glasses, they sit and groove, the soft rhythms of Marley and Burning Spear emanating from their blasters. They sit there in the certain knowledge that those two fat-thighed school teachers from Iowa or the lab technician from Hamburg who have been here two days already without seeing the real Jamaica and who are eager for the great experience on this one week out of a year of routine, will soon walk by to make some astute, conversation-creating comment about his carefully coiffed "dreadlocks" or about "raygay" music . . .

It rarely fails. In a few minutes, after Bertha Bigthighs and her friend

"Bob Marley was I personal idren."

Bess have luxuriated in the delicious feeling of danger and adventure, confident that no-one from their school district is likely to see them, they will circuitously wander by to "hear" the music for the first time and offer a friendly "Hi". Our hero grins invitingly, two gold teeth glinting: "Greetings to the daughters."The addressed, aged from 17 to 47 (the latter if it's a bad week), feel the delicious shiver running up their spines and, encouraged, begin to nod off-beat to the music. "Is that raygay?" the more extroverted and insightful asks, and completes the code by referring to her only frame of reference, "Is that Bob Marlay?" Our hero concurs or demurs, and quietly briefs them on Bob Marley who was his personal idren or Burning Spear, another personal idren. His casual, conversation-making questioning begins. "Where the daughters hail from?" The Iowans respond. Our hero calculates - silently. Iowa is, as far as he figures, quite some way off from New York, which is where he plans to take up residence, given friendly assistance in the securing of a visa. Iowa sounds like the Mocho (the back-a-bush district) of the U.S.A. Still, he needs sneakers, his girlfriend is on his case about a chain . . . The Iowans will do until his New York lady comes along. He casually tosses his locks and the goose-pimples begin for the Iowans. Soon they are off, listening to learned discourses on Rastafari, an invitation to a fish and bammy feed. They drink it all in enthralled. Excitement. Bertha beams. Can the Big Bamboo be far behind?

THE TOURIST

There has very recently been a major move afoot to bring increasingly large numbers of tourists to the shores of our lovely little island. Unfortunately, however, many tourists arrive unprepared. Listed below is a guide to the prerequisites for becoming the Complete Jamaican Tourist.

i) A few US dollars which translate into many devalued Jamaican dollars.
ii) Skimpy swimwear - designed to give maximum exposure.
iii) Large straw sun hat.
iv) Permanent smile.
v) 35 mm still camera - for capturing native beauty.

Seeing Jamaica like a native

"Nice lady, buy something from me!"

vi) VHS Video camera - for capturing native beauty in motion.

vii) Money - to pay for privilege of photographing native beauty.

viii) Tape recorder - for sampling exotic native music.

ix) Brightly coloured floral shorts.

x) T-shirt printed in Jamaica.

xi) Sandals to be worn with socks - never without.

xii) Burnt "cherry red" nose with white calamine lotion applied.

xiii) Sunglasses perched on above.

xiv) Suntan lotion.

xv) The ability to start all conversations with the line "What a lovely Island!"

xvi) The ability to end all conversations with the line "I don't know why anyone would want to leave this lovely Island."

xvii) Straw basket with bright raffia design usually made in Hong Kong.

xviii) Stick of sensemelia - to be used for medicinal purposes only, of course.

xix) The ability to steadfastly avoid sampling native sexual delights except of course for research and/or diplomacy.

xx) Scotch tape - water resistant - for strapping ganja to the body - especially useful at time of Departure.

xxi) Synthetic dread locks a la Bo Derek.

xxii) The ability to carefully avoid harassing the natives.

xxiii) The physical attribute that allows one to perspire profusely.

xxiv) The ability to keep a straight face on hearing "Yellow Bird" for the 105th time during one's six-day vacation.

xxv) The ability to dance without a sense of rhythm.

xxvi) The ability to sit through six nights of native floor shows featuring limbo dancers and fire eaters during one's six-day vacation.

xxvii) The ability to avoid being harassed (*see North Coast Hustler*).

THE RASTAFARIAN

No category of Jamaican is more devout or righteous than the Rastafarian - as he will be sure to tell you (directly or indirectly). Rastafarianism is a serious business. Don't be confused by all those imposter dreadlocks who are out there commiting all sorts of abominations. **True** Rastas merely tolerate Babylon. The true Rasta spends his time waiting it out, enduring the immoral, corrupt, decadent Crazy Baldheads (non-Rastas) that encircle him like peel-head John Crows, as he waits to go back to Africa.

Mind you, how you define "waiting it out" depends on which sect you belong to. One species waits it out by making brooms while scanning the horizon for the ships that are going to take him back to his Homeland (Ethiopia). Another species, on the other hand, will probably be waiting it out by playing football or playing reggae or playing with the BMW

or Volvo that he bought with the proceeds of playing football or playing reggae.

No matter what the species, though, all Rastas love to pass the waiting-it-out time by "reasoning". And this is decidedly a most successful way of disposing of very many hours. Reasoning is so complex and profound that it might take an entire night for a bredren to get a single point across. Do you find it difficult to follow his flow of logic? Ah, that's because you haven't partaken of the "Sacrament". Take a draw from the chalice (the pipe) ... take a **long, long** draw. There: see how everything makes sense now?

Note that the above discourse refers to "he" rather than 'he or she'. This is not to say that all Rastas are male. By no means. However, the female Rasta is content to walk three steps

44

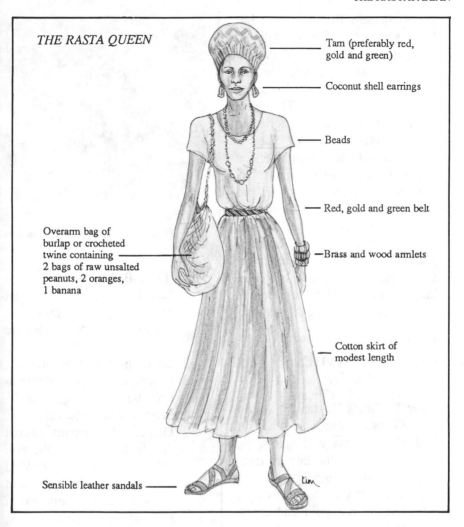

THE RASTA QUEEN

Tam (preferably red, gold and green)

Coconut shell earrings

Beads

Red, gold and green belt

Brass and wood armlets

Overarm bag of burlap or crocheted twine containing 2 bags of raw unsalted peanuts, 2 oranges, 1 banana

Cotton skirt of modest length

Sensible leather sandals

behind, being fully aware of her inferior status. The Rasta Queen knows that her main role in life is to care for her King and service his needs, by cooking, cleaning and producing baby Rastas (attired, of course, in ankle-length robes which her King has deemed appropriately modest). Of the three activities, she is probably least productive in the former (since for at least one week out of

every month her King ordains that all such activities must cease), and most productive in the latter (in which her King gives her free reign - absolutely no hindrances, no encumbrances, no barriers of any sort, if you get our drift). So, greatly encouraged by her King, the Queen goes ahead and produces one, two, three, four, five, six children. Is she, on the birth of number seven, surprised to hear that her King has been seen around town with an indecently clad bun-head gal (or on the north coast, female tourist), on the back of his motorbike? Of course not. The wise Queen understands that her even wiser King, now assured that she is anchored seven-fold on a Straight and Righteous path, has generously decided to go out and rescue one of the Children of Babylon. And see, within months she is proven right: the bun-head gal has stopped wearing make-up and started wearing a tie-head and long skirt. Ah, Jah be praised. Another convert along the way.

PHYSICAL CHARACTERISTICS OF THE RASTA

How To Dress Rasta:
1. Grow dreadlocks.
2. (The above will take some time, so in the interim conceal the ungodly state of your head by the following:) wear a red, gold and green tam.
3. If female, always cover your hair, wear modest high-necked tops and long, flowing skirts.
4. If male, you may wear anything except long, flowing skirts.
5. Neither male nor female is advised to wear make-up.
6. Cultivate a gaunt, stringy look by adopting a salt-free diet and eschewing (n.b. not

"Locks"

chewing) all meat, **especially** pork.

How To Talk Rasta:
1. Learn to expound, at great length (e.g. 2-3 hours), on the true meaning of obscure passages in the Bible.
2. Learn to speak in parables.
3. Punctuate all your declarations with "Jah! Ras-Tafari!"
4. Learn Rasta language:
   Delete all pronouns except "I" from your vocabulary. "I" may now be sprinkled liberally in all sentences and permutated and combined in all sorts of exciting ways, e.g.:

I-man:	*I, me, myself, my*
the I:	*You, your*
I and I:	*We, us, our*
I-dren:	*bredren (brethren)*
I-tal:	*vital*
I-rie:	*okay*

Names may also easily be made more righteous, e.g. I-Rol (Errol), I-Roy (Leroy), I-Kael (Michael), I-ny (Tony), etc., etc.

THE JAMAICAN FAMILY

DEFINITION - PLAYERS AND FUNCTIONS

The mother
- *Gives birth*

The child
- *Is born*

The father
- *Disappears at the birth of the child*

The grandmother
- *Cares for children while mother goes off to New York/Toronto to bear another child.*

Yu daddy ain't yu daddy . . .

The Family Tree: Deeply Rooted and Intertwined.

The above definition of the Jamaican family serves two purposes:

a) to indicate the major players and
b) to introduce the endless possibilities of kinship ties.

It is not uncommon for one to encounter a third cousin on one's stepfather's half brother's sister's side. Similarly there is a relatively high occurrence of great aunts and great uncles on one's mother's boyfriend's father-in-law's side.

Such permutations have led to the development of the many branched "family tree" - a tree that extends its branches into every inhabitable corner of the earth. For instance it is quite usual for a Jamaican to meet his English cousin while visiting his Chinese half sister at his Barbadian father's house in the Tibetan highlands.

The benefits from this kind of abundant foliage are many - just think, because one's extended family could be anyone, any and everywhere: when travelling, free accommodation and meals are available worldwide.

Part II

It's Like This . . .

JAMAICANS AND RELIGION

Indisputably, Jamaicans are a religious people. Unofficial estimates have even put the number of churches ahead of the number of bars - no mean feat. Sensibly though, Jamaicans scrupulously compartmentalize their lives. As they are fond of repeating, "There's a time and place for everything" . . . In this matter, religious activity is not allowed to spill over into one's personal life to any great extent. Religion, i.e. going to church, is a Sunday activity. The rest of the week, as illustrated by the number of bars, is for other things.

Which should not be held to imply insincerity. Anyone who staggers in, inebriated, at 5:30 a.m. Sunday morning after a taxing night on the town, and struggles into formal wear to head out to church at 7:00 a.m. as does many a Jamaican, is unqualifiedly serious. The young man in the back pew, his eyes screwed shut, may or may not be experiencing spiritual bliss: his posture may be motivated by piety. Equally he may be trying to hold his head together.

The truth is that the Jamaican capacity for riotous living is only exceeded by his need to feel guilty. As befits one who has been brought up in a staunchly protestant milieu, peopled by fire-and-brimstone ecclesiastics, he **knows** that having had so much fun is bad for him. And until, hungover on a Sunday morning, he has had his head assaulted by an over-amplified preacher, damning him and his vile offspring to perdition, he cannot relax.

With so many weekday sinners, it is no wonder then

All in the Spirit Business.

that religion is a prime growth area. There is nothing unusual about one day seeing a tent go up on a corner lot anywhere in the country, and in another week seeing it replaced by steel girders and cement blocks until, a month or so later, depending on the pace of contributions from the faithful, a new palatial church emerges.

(Indeed one irreverent song, titled "Pitch a Tent", suggested that if things got bad and one couldn't pay one's rent, a solution would be to pitch a tent on the nearest lot and start a church. The un-amused authorities promptly banned it from airplay.)

Notwithstanding their religious nature (which we know must be true because our politicians say it every week) Jamaicans have not, given their penchant for harmless humour, spared the religious authority from their good-natured ribbing. For instance, Jamaican preachers are held to be particularly gifted at the "laying on of hands" particularly where the church sisters are concerned. Somehow, the deacon always seems to be singled out: legendary tales of erring deacons making miraculous exits from bedrooms where they were innocently hearing confessions and offering counsel, or of

51

deacons who, out of duty, have suggested that certain sisters stay behind late at church to do some extra prayer, circulate through the society. And it is noticeable that the majority of church-goers, particularly those at late night services, are women. Of course there is nothing of credibility behind such stories.

To seriously suggest other-wise does us a great dis-service.

THE JAMAICAN
POPULAR MUSIC SCENE

THE PLAYERS

Star:

Any singer or deejay who has 'cut' his first tune. Record companies are fighting over him, women are rushing him and going mad over him. Considers himself the natural successor to Bob Marley. Victim of conspiracy hatched by "dem". His "conscious" lyrics are aimed at the upliftment of the oppressed and at making the first instalment on his new BMW or Benz. Wears locks, or, if hair refuses to grow, tam. After two hits he migrates to London or New York.

Would-be Star:

Every other Jamaican male between 11 and 35. He thinks the star has sold out. He has the tune that will make Jamaicans walk and talk to themselves, but is also a victim of "dem". Seen hanging out at recording studios, heard singing on every street corner of the country.

Producer:

Drives a Benz or BMW. Knows little or no music. Favourite phrases are "Check me tomorrow", and "This contract is just a formality. Put your mark here". He is also sadly misunderstood by artistes who absurdly believe that he printed up twice the number of records that he acknowledges. See also, "dem".

Band:

Any group of friends who have mastered three chords on guitar and bass.

Deejay:

Recording artiste who never made it into the school choir in his youth and has held a grudge against society ever since. Believes creativity is an elitist affectation. A "riddim" that has worked for fifty years is good enough. Keen sense of irony, shown in his preference for martial and macho names e.g. "Brigadier", "General", "Lone Ranger", etc. while chanting "cultural", "uplifting", "conscious", "peaceful" and "righteous" lyrics, off-key. See "Star".

Radio Deejay:
Allegedly accepts money for playing alleged music. U.S. accent. See also "dem".

"Dem":
Oligarchy comprised of producers, radio deejays, politicians, etc., who conspire to fight down all conscious artistes by denying them airplay, studio time and millions of dollars of royalties.

Promoter:
Stages the year's top show every other month. Shows are promoted on the basis of an advertised line-up of twenty top stars, ten of whom have actually been booked for the show and five of whom will actually appear.

Emcee:
His primary function at shows is to dream up

novel reasons why half the acts have not appeared and why the show is two hours late. This information is usually conveyed in an American accent.

THE SHOW

Most stage shows are billed to start at 8:00 - 8:30 p.m. In most cases though, the advance party of soundmen, lightsmen, security guards, pickpockets and purveyors of bogus tickets take up their positions by 6:00 p.m. The gates open an hour later. The show may begin by 10:00 p.m., what with the overselling of tickets by the promoter, bogus tickets, the generosity of security guards in allowing the entry of ticketless persons at a below-the-table half price, the expertise of the beating-the-gate habitues and the hordes of hangers-on that the performers insist must be allowed free entry.

Beating the gate, it should be noted, is a sacrosanct tradition. Just as few self respecting Jamaican showgoers will join a queue when there is an opportunity to bump and bore, so too will few showgoers pay to enter if they can beat the gate. A gate-beating aficionado will walk two miles around to the back of the site, rip his clothes to scale a wall or

"Love and Harmony"

squeeze through barbed wire to avoid the levy. The influx of guard dogs has only added another challenge. True aficionados will beat the gate and turn around and leave immediately.

Lyrics:
Listener's perspective:
  Incomprehensible
DJ's/singers' perspective:
  Conscious, righteous
  etc.
For example:
Goodbye goodbye . . .
   bye . . . bye
Don't want no W-A-R
Don't want to go F-A-R
Cause my baby's L-A-T-E
And she will not W-A-T-E
Chorus:
  Haul and pull up
  Do it rockers styley
  Haul and pull up
  Do it wicked and wiley
  etc., etc., etc.

DANCE HALL DAZE

First popularized in the late fifties and early sixties, the Dance Hall phenomenon has surfaced again in the mid-eighties, though with some unfortunate modifications. Earlier, unlike today, very little live music was used. Then too, one of the most endearing features of that period, the rent-a-tile, has virtually died out. (For the uninitiated, rent-a-tile explored the degree of movement vertically, horizontally and laterally, possible to a couple dancing on a six-inch square tile.) Its offspring, the dub, a more aggressive style and with motion confined to the pelvic area (as in "Me say, a dub out her blouse an skirt") has in turn given way to a no contact free style form of dancing. Boring.

55

JAMAICAN MEDICINES AND PRESCRIPTIONS

Jamaicans are fascinated by illnesses and cures. They realize, astutely, that the latter do not necessarily relate to the former. To know a Jamaican for twenty- five minutes is to know, in precise detail, his or her medical history. In another five, he or she will diagnose yours.

We are no ordinary hypochondriacs. What we can boast is a propensity towards certain types of illnesses that are, shall we say, unusual. So, it must be said, are the cures.

For instance, in no other country do "colds" or "gas" affect so great a number of its population. In the case of the latter, its widespread nature due to our surfeit of politicians might be expected. Nonetheless, it transcends that breed.

Where else, for instance, would you find spontaneous admission and acceptance of "gas" in the eye, nose, throat, forehead, kidney, liver, knee and toe? Or, "colds" in the ankle, ear, finger, hip and sole of the foot?

Jamaicans eagerly swap tales of "sugar" (diabetes), blood pressure (always too high), and compete with each other to list which family lost more members to cancer, strokes, or heart failure.

The surefire cures are the centrepiece of these tales. Every Jamaican over 25 (for, alas, the young have little respect for tradition and accumulated wisdom) knows a dozen or more cures for ostensibly serious illnesses. The problem is though, what is conclusively held to be a cure in rural Westmoreland, may, in southern Portland, be conclusively known as a contributor to the illness and vice versa.

Still, there are areas of unanimity. Cerassee tea, for instance, is

56

reputed to solve menstrual cramps, backaches caused by concupiscence, headaches, chest pains among others. Many will attest to the fact that many such illnesses disappear even at the very mention of the name. It is not a pleasant tasting brew.

"Sinkle bible", perhaps the only herbal application that remotely approaches the foulness of cerassee tea, is held to be good for healing cuts and for curing children of thumbsucking. It is also widely administered to animals as a remedy (with honey) for diarrhoea and miscarriages.

Thousands of children, former sufferers of whooping cough, can attest to the efficacy of a broth made from parts of rats (who cares which parts). Some have survived into adulthood.

Never a nation of people to seek the middle ground when there are extreme positions to be taken, Jamaican families of rural origin place great store on washouts, a cleansing of the system aided by castor oil that, practised by the over-zealous, has kept many hospital beds occupied.

Certain medicinal concoctions are, though illegal, widely used. For instance, various balmyards ruled by Brother This or Sister That, who will vehemently deny that they are practitioners of obeah, will prescribe "Oil of Turn Back", "Oil of Desire", "Oil-of-Severe-Illness-to-the-Deceitful-and-Wicked-Transgressors" etc., with obvious intent. Some are to be ingested by the client, others by the proposed victim. So potent are some of these brews that one renowned Brother set up a car-repair shop next door to his practice as he found out that one elixir was dynamite in removing paint from car bodies.

Given the high Jamaican interest in acquiring visas to North America, certain entrepreneurial-minded and innovative balmyard practitioners have devised special prescriptions for the fateful interview with the Consular Officers. These may range from the (mild) suggestion that certain colours be worn (both inner and outer garments) or the (potent) advice that one's passport be soaked in six-day-old urine over which certain chants have been read. There is evidence that the potency of this prescription is being felt in the embassies. One has recently put up a sign saying "Please keep your passport dry".

Importantly, many urban Jamaicans publicly ridicule such "superstitious foolishness". Not a few, however, are thought to hurry indoors immediately after such words have passed their lips, to burn a few candles to ward off retribution. In any case, unless the

"What will it put back?"

lower-income folks, held to be the prime believers in balmyard activities, have suddenly acquired wealth, it is difficult to explain the many limousines that discreetly hover near these sites in the late evening, the time set aside for "private" ministrations. It has been suggested credibly though, that many politicians and lawyers have been incorrectly reported as visiting such institutions when it is known for a fact that there are so many look-alikes in this country.

Of course, being Jamaican, we place a lot of emphasis on medicinal and other brews that perpetuate sexual process. We borrowed the "Chinese Brush" and the Tantaria from elsewhere, to give sagging limbs a boost, but on our own, we've developed the "Front End Lifter" and "Irish Moss" which are doing very well, thank you.

DRIVING IN JAMAICA

The Jamaican Driver is a far-sighted and shrewd individual, who is constantly called upon to make important decisions quickly. For him the words diplomacy, dialogue and negotiation possess a special kind of significance.

Very early in his life as a Driver, this individual is called upon to test his skills to the maximum, beginning with the driving test and continuing further in the area of motor vehicle licensing and certification. For it is here that he will meet the most zealously patriotic of examiners: men and women who will demand that he demonstrate a thorough knowledge of the value of the contribution of our nation's heroes (e.g. Busta, Manley . . . but most especially Sangster) to the efficient functioning of Jamaican society.

The scene of the accident is usually the place where the Driver is most thoroughly tested. It is here that the use of his skills in Dialogue and Negotiation must be proven to be up to scratch, especially so because it is here that he is working against time: he must concretize his case before the Police arrive.

SKILLS IN NEGOTIATION:

This may be defined as the ability to assemble a large crowd of eyewitnesses:-

i) all of whom actually saw the accident before it happened, as it was happening and after it happened,

ii) who will attest to the fact that you - the Driver - are not the kind of Driver or indeed the person to commit the infraction that is suggested by the other party,

iii) who will attest to having known you the Driver and your family from birth (it is of little significance where and when the Driver was born).

59

Motto of the National Pothole Dodgers Association:
"He that falleth in may ne'er be seen again."

This is no mean feat, especially when the accident occurred on an isolated strip of road with not a creature in sight.

SKILLS IN DIALOGUE:

Expertise in this field may be regarded as the most important of tools:

- Party (a) says to party (b) "You wrong".
- Party (b) says to party (a) "You wrong".
- Party (a) to party (b) "No you wrong".
- Party (b) to party (a) "No you wrong", etc.

It is believed that the term "Ye of quick tongue", was not, contrary to persistent popular belief, coined because of a sex-related activity but rather at the scene of an accident similar to the above. Let us at this point indicate that the Driver, "he of quick tongue", is merely responsible for getting the dialogue started; having done this, his faithful eyewitnesses, all of whom were at his house on the day of his birth, carry the dialogue to its logical conclusion.

Please note carefully that this kind of activity is highly recommended as a method to improve the ability of one's larynx and to magnificently enhance one's vocabulary of expletives.

The Minibus Passenger:
Willing to meet face to face, back to back, belly to belly.

SOME DEFINITIONS OF ROAD USERS

The Minibus:
The single instrument that brings the Jamaican masses together - very, very, very close together.

The Minibus Driver:
A truly misplaced individual who would really be more at home driving bumper cars at Coney Island or driving tanks around obstacle courses.

The Minibus Passenger:
One who is willing to meet others face to face, back to back, belly to belly.

The Rental:
Oh, if this car could speak.

The Rent-A-Car Driver:
Motto: "Faster than a speeding bullet".

The Taxi:
Totally defiant of the term "obsolete".

The Taxi Driver:
The only truly unpredictable and spontaneous driver on the road, willing to cut you off just to keep in practice for combat with minibuses.

The Private Vehicle Driver:
Lives in perpetual fear of being within 10 yards of rentals, minibuses and taxis.

The Mechanic:
Beware when he says "Thanks, do call again", he means it - he knows something that you don't.

The Pedestrian:
The ultimate chance taker.

HELPFUL TIPS

- When approaching a traffic light that's signalling red. . . cut through the gas station on the corner instead.

- When involved in an accident, always remember that it is not your fault.

- When a Learner Driver is in front of you, help him to sharpen his road responses by honking your horn, shouting expletives, or cutting in front of him.

- When turning left, right or stopping, don't bother to indicate. All Jamaicans love surprises.

- Never challenge a taxi or mini-bus unless you have a mechanic or a bodyman who can and will do your repairs, cheaply.

- To cross a pedestrian crossing during the day:
  a) Do it swiftly as if in a 100-meters dash
  b) Wait for a traffic jam - then cross
  c) If elderly, don't even consider it.

- The efficient road repair man works only from:
  8:00 a.m. to 10:00 a.m., and
  3:00 p.m. to 5:00 p.m.,
  Monday to Friday. He must be expert at handling a flag in a manner to cause traffic jams.

Always keep cool.

WHO DRIVES WHAT?

* Ganja barons and reggae stars drive brand new BMW's and Benzes.

* Prominent doctors and lawyers drive Volvos.

* Successful businessmen drive brand new Isuzus (Company cars).

* Yuppies drive brand new Accords (Company cars).

* Government ministers' bodyguards drive black cars with black-tinted windows.

* I.C.I.'s (also known as Higglers) drive Mercedes Benzes.

* Evangelist-preachers drive Accords Monday to Saturday, and Benzes on Sundays.

* Rankins and Ganja Gophers drive Rentals.

* Mechanics drive 1970 Cortinas.

* University Lecturers drive 1968 VWs.

* School teachers take mini-buses.

GENERAL RULES/ GUIDELINES

● Only ganja barons, higglers, reggae stars, government ministers, successful businessmen and yuppies drive new cars.

● Only ganja barons and higglers drive their **own** new cars.

● Only ganja barons and higglers buy new cars **and** new houses (paid for with cash).

● Japanese cars are in. European cars costing less than $1 million (estimated, probably more by time of publication) are out.

● Rental licence plates are in. Cars with rental licence plates that are actually rented are out.

● Unaffordable cars are in. Affordable cars are out.

● Car mechanics are in. Car salesmen are out.

DEALING WITH
JAMAICAN GOVERNMENT OFFICIALS
(TIPS)

MEETINGS:

These are the main activities of officials, and ground rules apply. Meetings should never be scheduled before ten a.m. (ungodly time) unless it's a breakfast meeting which can begin as early as the nearest hotel opens and which may go on until 11:00 a.m. Meetings are also out of the question between noon and three unless they are luncheon meetings, and of course, never after 5:00 p.m., unless it's a meeting over drinks or at dinner. You, of course, are expected to pick up the bill.

APPOINTMENTS:

Notwithstanding the above, all appointments with officials are, essentially, theoretical. For instance, a 10:30 a.m. appointment is not expected to be honoured before 11:00 a.m. because the official is attending another meeting from which he'll hurry (if it's not a breakfast meeting) only to tell you that he has another appointment in five minutes. However, don't be late for the **given** time. That shows a lack of consideration for **his** time, and he'll regretfully suggest another meeting at the first available slot in his diary two months hence.

FAVOURITE PHRASES OF GOVERNMENT OFFICIALS:

- "Can you call back again next week?"
- "That is what the regulation says."
- "I'm at lunch."
- "Yes, Mr. Minister. At once, Sir."
- "You have to fill out this form, take it up to ..... Street for stamping, then back here. And I close here in ten minutes."

"I can guarantee you will see him just before elections!"

BRIBES:

Perish the thought. Anyone crass enough to suggest a bribe deserves all the hassle he'll inevitably get. Tasty gifts show much better form.

OFFICE AMBIENCE:

Never be misled into believing that the reason why you cannot get someone's attention in a government institution is because, as it may appear, there are assorted groups gossiping, exchanging race track information or chatting to friends on the phone. What they are really doing is . . . never mind.

(a) **Items to be found in a junior official's desk**
- Betting sheet.
- Egg sandwich.
- Pornographic literature.

(b) **Items to be found in a middle level official's desk**
- Articles of association for the new company he's setting up.
- Key to the apartment in which he's installed his girlfriend.
- Pep pills.

(c) **Items to be found in a senior official's desk**
- Everything under (a) and (b) except that he has the keys to two apartments and twice as many pep pills.
- Stock market report.

SERVICE WITH A SMILE

(How to Serve Jamaican Style)

Jamaica is renowned for its extraordinary quality of service. Our island has carefully cultivated a particular type of attitude in its sales clerks, taxi drivers, waiters and waitresses, and most especially its civil servants, which is like no other. Many foreigners, and indeed some backward Jamaicans, have been taken aback by our unique style, and have struggled long and hard (but usually unsuccessfully) to acquire the technique. Have you succeeded, dear reader? To find out, take this simple test.

1. You are a sales clerk behind the counter in a large department store. A customer approaches, and stands there waiting to be served. You:
   a) Rush over to the customer with a sweet smile and offer assistance.
   b) Call another sales clerk from the other end of the store and ask him to assist the customer.

   c) Pick up the phone and dial a girlfriend to hear what happened on Dynasty last night.

2. You are a waitress in a respectable uptown restaurant. Someone whom you have just served complains that there's a fly in his soup. You:
   a) Apologise profusely, rush off to replace the soup, and insist that his entire meal be on the house.
   b) Insist that he show you the fly before you reluctantly replace the soup.
   c) Give him a withering cut-eye, kiss your teeth and then walk off haughtily.

3. You are a Post Office employee, responsible for selling stamps. It has been a quiet morning but at 11:45 a.m., fifteen minutes before your lunch break, a crowd of a dozen people suddenly converges on your line. You:

"So what happened on Dynasty last night?"

a) Serve them all quickly, so that you are able to go to lunch at 12:05.

b) Serve them at your usual slow pace, then close the cage precisely at 12:00, leaving six of them standing there.

c) Amble off immediately, muttering about finding a package only loudly enough that the people at the front of the line can hear . . . then at 12:05, ask a co-worker to go and advise the people to join another line if they want to be served because you're at lunch.

4. You are a telephone operator, on a night shift. The phone rings at midnight. A hysterical woman tells you that someone is trying to break into her house, but she has been unable to reach the police. You:

a) Promptly take down her name and address, then yourself contact the police.

b) Tell her you wish you could help, but you're about to take a coffee break.

c) The question is irrelevant, since you never pick up the phone under any circumstances after 11:00 p.m.

5. You are an air stewardess on a flight of your national airline. The flight is particularly hectic, being full of I.C.I.'s. One I.C.I. complains of feeling faint and requests a glass of water. You:
   a) Rush up to her with water and smelling salts.
   b) Tell her you'll soon come.
   c) Complain loudly to a fellow stewardess that these damn people keep harassing you every minute, then flounce off in the opposite direction.

6. You are a bellboy in a north coast hotel. A departing American guest with six heavy suitcases tells you, while waving a U.S. ten dollar bill, that he needs you to run with all six suitcases to the bus **immediately**, as it is about to leave the compound. You:
   a) Suggest tactfully that it might work better if you ask the bus driver to hang on a minute while you get the trolley.
   b) Smile and tell him, in an American accent, "No problem!"
   c) Tell him you've only got two hands.

ANSWERS:

**1 (c), 2 (c), 3 (c),
4 (c), 5 (c), 6 (b).**

JAMAICAN EXCUSES

An immensely creative people, Jamaicans are very proud of their ability to think on their feet. Perhaps nowhere is this more evident than in their split-second ability to concoct excuses. While, as elsewhere, a major motive of excuse-making is to escape implicit or explicit criticism for some things done (or not done), many of our practitioners indulge simply, so to speak, to keep their hand in.

Thus, even in cases where legitimate and perfectly acceptable (but boring) reasons for acts of omission or commission exist, a good practitioner feels duty bound to creatively embellish.

69

"Are you telling me your mother died, again? How many lives does she have?"

Some grounds for excuses, and the explanations advanced, will include:

ON THE JOB

● *Absence from work*

My - mother
   - father
   - son
   - grandmother's third
      cousin's auntie's
      step child by my
      father's side
   - dog
(You get the drift)

   - died yesterday
   - was buried yesterday
   - is in hospital
   - had a heart attack
   - was hit by a drunken
      driver who ran a stop
      light as he was being
      chased by the police

● *Lateness for work*

my car/the   - was stopped
minibus   in a roadblock
               - broke down
               - was seized by
                  the police
               - was in a minor
                  accident while
                  trying to avoid
                  hitting a little
                  child chasing
                  his ball across
                  the road

70

"This mad woman held me down!"

AT HOME

- **Husband sneaks in at 3:30 a.m and finds screw-faced wife waiting**

  (sweetheart   "I tried to call you
  (honey   but the phone at
  (darling   the bedside of
  (babes   my hospitalized
  (sweets   friend wasn't
                   working."

  "I know you won't believe this but we sat down at the office trying to put a paper together for a presentation today and none of us realized the time."

  "I know you're not really planning to use that gun."

- **Wife catches husband in bed with another woman**

  (sweetheart   "I'm so glad you
  (honey   came. This mad
  (darling   woman just held
  (babes   me down."
  (sweets

  "I thought I was in bed with you. So who is this vile imposter?"

SOME POINTS TO NOTE:

- Keep track of your family tree. Some over-zealous personnel officer is likely to recall that your mother had earlier died two years ago. With the typical Jamaican extended family, you are on better grounds with an in-law or half-cousin.

- Inanimate objects are acceptable as antagonists and are thus plausible excuses for happenstances. e.g. the bed fell on my foot; the fridge nearly electrocuted me.

71

VERANDAH TALK

By repute, the art of verandah talk was most avidly practised by the housewives of Upper St. Andrew. For the uninitiated, this form of social intercourse involves the airing (and creative modification) of matters of major national importance, e.g. who's making it with whom, how well and how often, when and where. As the story goes, these housewives were the ones who could afford to spend hours sipping tea (pinkies askew) and nibbling biscuits while discreetly passing on information always prefaced by

"My dear chile, did you hear . . ."

Politricks: A favourite Verandah Talk topic.

"My dear, did you **know (hear)** that . . .?"; information that largely concerned members of their own class.

Now, however, it is evident that Jamaica has experienced the verandahization of the entire society. It is now taken as fact that it is on the verandahs of Jamaica that the movers and shakers of society make the decisions that are later formalized in mock debates and discussions in Parliament and in corporate boardrooms. More interestingly, though, in keeping with its genteel forbears, it is on Jamaica's verandahs that the nation's GNP (Grossest National Product), Scandal and Slander, is planted, nurtured and disseminated.

The transformation has given the lie to the long-held belief that gossip is the prerogative of the female. The most efficient verandah talkers, those whose juicy offerings form the diet of innuendo for radio call-in programmes and discreet letters of enquiry in the newspapers, are men. Characteristically they drop

73

in on their friends for a few minutes, plant a suspicion and are off to the next verandah. In three hours' time, phones from Morant Point to Negril are abuzz with the news of which Government Minister's ganja shipment was hijacked, which police officer demanded a half-million dollars to hush up an orgy that got out of hand . . . no matter how private an arrangement was, it will be on the verandah within a few hours.

FAVOURITE VERANDAH TOPICS

Sex:

Primary discussion point. Jamaicans acknowledge that sex - not love nor money - makes the world go round. Thus the sex lives of politicians, religious figures, captains of industry and other assorted charlatans are minutely examined. Jamaicans tend to suspect leaders who eschew a vigorous sex life, and some leaders of less than average prowess have been suspected of attempting to plant larger-than-life tales that they later attempt, with due modesty, to deny.

Politics:

This, a sometimes boring diversion, nonetheless features prominently. Verandah talk itemizes conclusively the reasons behind seemingly above-board legislation, which MP's are out or in and who is angling for a political appointment. Often too, politicians, wary of public response, can either triumphantly introduce or vigoriously condemn programmes and policies that they themselves have planted.

Corruption:

Verandah talk is often not condemnatory. Helpful advice on the amount of bribes certain officials require, or the sources of illicit goods, is disseminated through the system. One may also learn the locale and size of various overseas bank accounts, the true owners of dummy corporations and which relative of which politician has received a lucrative government contract.

HOW TO
GET THINGS DONE
IN JAMAICA

A. Know the Right People, i.e.:
   a) Very rich people
   b) People who know very rich people
   c) Government Ministers
   d) Members of the Board of Directors within the organization where you're trying to get things done.

B. If you don't know the Right People, wrangle invitations to cocktail parties where the Right People are so you can get to know them.

C. Alternatively, **pretend** you know them. (Easy because the Right People are usually so egocentric that they assume everyone knows them.)

D. Alternatively, pretend to **others** that you know them, e.g.: *"Sorry, can't stop to chat, I'm on my way to Jamaica House."* Or: *"Percy says he wants me to help them out at the Ministry but chuh, I can't bother with them people, man."* Or: *"I was up at Jamaica House this morning and the P.M. says to me, 'Horace' -he calls me Horace, you know ..."*

E. Approach an underling (e.g. Junior Manager) and pretend you know **him** or **her** very well. (N.B. Some research is necessary if you use this method.) E.g.: Opening sentence: *"Wha' 'appen, Miss Campbell! How's the family?"* (Note that this opener will get you nowhere if (1) her name is not Miss Campbell, and (2) she has no family.) Then continue with: *"Did Missa Mac tell you about that matter?"* (Note that you have already discovered that McFarlane is the name of Miss Campbell's supervisor.) Needless to say, Miss Campbell has no idea what you're talking about. You have her at a disadvantage. Follow up on this immediately with: *"Oh . . ."* (hurt, disappointed) *"When he was at my house last night for dinner he said he was going to ask you to look about getting that telephone installed for me - today."* Done.

F. A simpler solution is to visit a balmyard - one with a reputation for guaranteed and quick results (an easy way to choose one is to stick to one of those frequented by the Right People themselves).

G. The simplest solution of all: "Let off" something, i.e., drop a "smalls" - a not-too-small amount of money, that is.

Construction work, at a restful pace.

HOW TO OPERATE UNDER
JAMAICA TIME

BASIC RULES:

1. Never show up anywhere on time - unless this is a deliberate ploy to flummox an adversary (who will of course arrive at the normal time, i.e. 15 minutes late).

2. 15 minutes late is standard procedure - except for particular events as stated below.

3. Try to arrive a respectable 10 minutes late to business meetings - unless you're a Director, in which case 45 minutes late is appropriate in order to impress your importance on the gathering.

Other guidelines:
Theatre:
　　10 minutes late
Cinema:
　　20 minutes late
Work:
　　29 minutes late (half an hour late is slackness)

Parties:
　　3 hours late (come any earlier and you'll be the first)
Reggae Concerts:
　　5 hours late.

GENERALLY:

● Arriving on time is regarded as over-zealous, if not indecent.

● Arriving up to 5 minutes early is taken as a deliberate ploy to antagonize.

● Arriving more than 5 minutes early is an obvious indication of:

　(a)　extreme idleness; or
　(b)　mental instability.

● Arriving 5 minutes late means super-efficiency.

● Arriving 10 minutes late means efficiency.

● Arriving 15 minutes late means you're normal.

77

- Arriving 20-30 minutes late may warrant your issuing a vague, casually muttered excuse, e.g.: "Bwoy, traffic heavy out there to rahtid!"

- Arriving over 30 minutes late will probably warrant a more specific excuse, e.g. "Sorry, I got 1/2/3 punctures on the way" (number depending on how late you are), or "Sorry, my car/my friend's car/the taxi/the minibus broke down" (ideal since this is an everyday occurrence for most Jamaicans, and also it accounts for a limitless delay). (See *Jamaican Excuses* for other possibilities.)

Buses operate under Jamaica Time.

PUNCTUALITY IS REQUIRED FOR:

- Funerals

- Weddings (unless you're the bride, in which case you are expected to arrive 30 minutes late)

- Work (for the first week on the job)

- Cricket

SOME TRANSLATIONS FOR THE NOVICE:

- "I'll be there in 5 minutes" means "I'll be there in 25 minutes".

- "I'll be there in a few minutes" means "I'll be there in 30/40/50 minutes".

- "I'll soon be there" means anywhere from 1 to 2 hours.

- "I'll come by later" means "I **might** come, and if so it will probably be just before you leave/go to bed/give up totally".

- "I'll do it later" means "I **may** do it tomorrow/next week/next year - if I feel like it".

- "Soon come" means "Don't hold your breath".

SOME TIMELESS JAMAICAN INSTITUTIONS:

JBC-TV:
An ace at precision, our No. 1 TV station takes pride in announcing its programme schedule in very specific terms, e.g. "approximately 7:42", "approximately 8:37" etc.

Needless to say the important part of that announcement is . . . guess which word.

AIR JAMAICA:
The on-time airline. When your flight will depart or arrive is anyone's guess (although the U.S. Government's Drug Enforcement Agency just **might** have an idea).

PRIME MINISTER'S SPEECH:
"The P.M. will deliver a message to the nation at 8:00 p.m." means that he **may** get started by 9:00 p.m.